Edgar Fawcett

Short Poems for Short People

Edgar Fawcett

Short Poems for Short People

ISBN/EAN: 9783744705516

Printed in Europe, USA, Canada, Australia, Japan

Cover: Foto ©Thomas Meinert / pixelio.de

More available books at **www.hansebooks.com**

SHORT POEMS

FOR

SHORT PEOPLE.

BY

EDGAR FAWCETT.

NEW YORK:

FRANCIS B. FELT & COMPANY,

91 MERCER STREET.

1872.

NOTE.

MANY of the poems in this volume have appeared in various magazines and journals throughout the country, previous to their present collection in book form. Permission to re-print a number of them has been obtained from Mr. Wm. Hayes Ward, of *The Independent*; Messrs. James R. Osgood & Co., of Boston; Messrs. Hurd & Houghton, of New York; Messrs. Davis & Elverson, of Philadelphia; Messrs. Lee & Shepard, of Boston; Mr. Frank Leslie, of New York; Mr. George S. Merriam, of New York; Mr. F. S. Street, of New York; Mr. Alfred Martien, of Philadelphia; Mr. W. H. Holbrooke, of New York; Mr. J. B. T. Marsh, of Cincinnati; Mrs. E. H. Miller, of Chicago; Mr. H. B. Fuller, of Boston; Mr. J. R. Elliott, of Boston, and Messrs. J. H. Carmany & Co., of San Francisco. The poems "Autumn" and "Santa Claus," were originally published in *Harper's Weekly;* "Under the Bedclothes," "An Awakening," "A School-Boy of the Period," first appeared in *Harper's Bazar;* "A School Girl of the Period," in *Harper's Magazine.*

DEDICATION.

If any girls or boys, whether American or English, can truthfully say of this little book, after having finished it, that the reading of what is written herein has given an hour of real, happy recreation, I pray that every such girl or boy shall believe the book to have been specially designed for her or for him, and to her or to him specially dedicated.

THE AUTHOR.

CONTENTS.

SHORT POEMS.

SENT TO BED.

I was n't a particle sleepy,
  And yet here I lie, all the same,
Sent straight off to bed when the clock struck nine;
  I think it 's a terrible shame!

Mamma is unfair in her treatment—
  There is n't a doubt of that truth;
Ruth Jones can sit up quite as late as she wants;
  Oh, dear, how I do envy Ruth!

They all were so gay in the parlor;
  Aunt Gertrude was singing a song,
And Uncle Joe just was commencing to tell
  That story he 's promised so long.

And brother Will, home for vacation,
  Was full of such capers and fun!

Mamma might have altered that hard rule of hers
  For one night, if only for one.

But no; as the clock began striking
  I happened to catch mamma's eye;
She first looked at me and then looked at the clock—
  'Twas easy to understand why.

And now I lie here in the darkness
  And silence, so solemn and deep.
Well, well, I *am* drowsy, the least little bit;
  There's nothing to *do* except sleep.

BABY'S BATH.

I THINK there never was so brave a baby
  In all the realms of Babydom, till now.
He positively looks upon cold water
  As something quite enjoyable, I vow.
The little pink-limbed atom of perfection!
  Just listen how melodiously he coos,
And reaches for the sponge Mamma is holding,
  As if she only meant it to amuse.

His playful hands are lightly dropt and lifted
  Like playful peach-blooms in some merry breeze,

And, oh, it is delight to watch the dimples
  That deepen if he bends his chubby knees!
Then, too, his low, soft laughter, never silent,
  His eyes more beautiful than evening-stars;—
Were only other babies half so docile,
  What comfort for a million poor mammas!

And when his bath is ended and I sing him,
  Rocked in his cosy cradle to and fro,
All gently, like the waving of a poppy,
  The sweetest of the lullabies I know,
How willingly his eyelids yield to slumber,
  What peace on dewy lips and pearly brow!
I think there never was so dear a baby,
  In all the realms of Babydom till now!

THE GOOD GIRL OVER THE WAY.

THERE once was a time when Mamma used to think
  I was tidy, obedient, clever;
But now it is useless to seek for her praise:
  She never bestows any—never!
My manners, my neatness, my talents, my dress,
  In short, all I do or I say,
By force of comparison suffers eclipse
  From the good girl over the way.

That girl is a mystery harder to solve
   Than my algebra's toughest equation,
Performing each duty in life with contempt
   For the slightest approach to evasion.
A flesh-and-blood piece of perfection, and made
   Of finer original clay,
What right have inferior mortals to rank
   With the good girl over the way?

Her virtues would fill quite a volume : at school
   She obtains all receivable medals,
Her management of the piano, I 've heard,
   Is a queenship of keys and pedals ;
Her worst composition is worthy of print,
   French verbs she considers mere play ;
And as for Geometry, Euclid was dull
   To the good girl over the way.

Now I, who am favored with fair common-sense,
   In my studies by no means deficient,
Dislike to encounter incessant rebuke
   For simply not being omniscient.
My mind is made up ; I shall certainly cease
   All further attempt, from to-day,
To copy those wonderful traits that exist
   In the good girl over the way.

Besides, it was only last evening I heard—
   Who told me of course does n't matter ;

The person, I have not a doubt, was sincere,
  And never intended to flatter—
Yes, only last evening I really heard
  O *such* a nice somebody say
That one of my smiles would be worth a whole kiss
  From the good girl over the way!

THE FIRST PANTS.

My pants are becoming,
    Beyond the least doubt,
But then I 'm a little
    Ashamed to go out.
I wonder if people
    Will stare when they see ;
I 'm certain Frank Harris
    Will make fun of me.

Well, Frank, if he chooses,
    May giggle and stare,
He 'd like it, I 'm certain,
    If *he* had a pair.
To-morrow at school, though,
    They 'll just hoot outright ;
But the first boy that touches me
    Gets in a fight.

I 'd like it much better
  To feel the least bit
As if these new trousers
  Were more of a fit.
It certainly is n't
  A thing to amuse,
This singular flapping
  I have round my shoes.

But, pshaw! by to-morrow
  They won't seem the same;
· I 'll quite have recovered
  From any false shame.
My last pants were nothing
  But poor little halves;
How odd if I *did n't*
  Feel loose in the calves!

A WAIL.

I SOMEHOW think my fate a very sad one;
  I 've not my rightful share of earthly joy,
Doomed as I am, through all my future life-time,
  To sorrow that I was n't born a boy.

I 've tried so hard to care for dolls, like most girls;
  But no, they don't amuse me one wee mite.

There 's nothing to my fancy half so lovely
 As just to spin a top or fly a kite.

I often watch, beside my bedroom window,
 The merry, jolly boys that romp and race,
When school is over, in the street beneath me,
 And wish that one of them could take my place.

Mamma considers me an awful creature,
 Papa believes me made but to annoy.
Of course it must be very, very dreadful,
 To have a child that 's neither girl nor boy.

But, then, am I to blame?   It 's hard to think so.
 A blind man cannot see without his eyes,
Nor yet a cripple walk without his crutches,
 No matter how much either of them tries.

And so the only thing that 's truly left me,
 Is to conclude my lot of earthly joy
Does n't compare at all with other people's,
 Lamenting that I was n't born a boy !

BEGINNING YOUNG.

Did I have a nice time at the party?
  Well, rather, Mamma; but you see,
The boys, from the smallest to largest,
  Were timid as timid could be.

Boys always are silly at parties;
  I wonder why girls always act
With twice as much manners and breeding?
  It seems a remarkable fact.

I saw *such* a nice little fellow,
  With glossy brown curls, there to-night;
His face would have made a sweet picture,
  So pleasant and rosy and bright.

But, then, he was awfully bashful,
  This boy with the brown curly hair;
I don't think he spoke the whole evening;
  The poor little soul did n't dare.

I liked him, but somehow it vexed me
  To have him sit still and not speak;
I 'm sure 't would have given me pleasure
  Right sharply to slap his plump cheek.

I punished him well by-and-by, though ;
  Don't tell it, Mamma, if you please ;
But, oh, what a kiss I did give him,
  Poor darling, in Pillows and Keys !

MY LITTLE ONE:

A PRAYER.

GOD bless my little one ! How fair
The mellow lamp-light gilds his hair,
Loose on the cradle-pillow there !—
God bless my little one !

God guard my little one !· To me
Life widowed of his life would be
As sea-sands widowed of the sea !—
God guard my little one !

God love my little one ! As clear
Cool sunshine holds the first green spear
On April meadows, hold him dear !—
God love my little one !

When these fond lips are mute, and when
I slumber, not to wake again,
God bless, God guard, God love him, then,
My little one ! Amen.

A SAD CASE.

I CAN'T understand why we don't like the things
    It 's wholesome and proper to eat ;
I wish that I just hated candies and cakes,
    And cared for potatoes and meat.

It frightens me, sometimes, to think what I 'd do,
    If only I had my own way
In a candy-shop or a baker-shop,
    With no one to watch me, some day.

For if any one left me alone with a lot
    Of candies and cakes at my side,
I firmly believe I should eat, and should eat,
    And should eat, and should eat, till I died.

CARRY'S TROUBLES.

DEMURE litttle Carry, eleven to-day,
    Has a world of annoyances, truly ,
Assuming the charge, in a sisterly way,
Of venturesome Kitty and mischievous May,
    And bold Master Max, the unruly.

Of course there is nurse to decide what is best,
   In cases of reckless resistance ;
But if nurse is the captain it must be confessed
That Carry affords, with unwearying zest,
   A corporal's watchful assistance.

When Kitty was found up the pear-tree, last week,
   With skirts in the branches entangled,
How long but for Carry's most opportune shriek,
Beholding the sister she wandered to seek,
   Would Kitty, head-downwards, have dangled ?

And May, fairy May, with her curls' glossy gold,
   And the brown eyes glimmering under,
Were it not for the hand-clasp so firm to hold,
From her restless gypseyings manifold
   Would she come back as safe, I wonder ?

And Max—what so hazardous he would not dare,
   All peril disdaining sublimely,
If somehow a hand were not always just there,
Intent upon saving Papa's son and heir
   In time, from an end most untimely ?

Poor Carry laments, now and then, that her days
   Are troubled—with good reason, truly !
And yet, how the love which they bear her repays
For all Kitty's pranks and all mischief of May's,
   All capers of Max, the unruly.

ABOVE ALL PRICE.

How dear does mother hold
   Her bonny little one?
Just as dear as the jostling clovers
   Hold the merry sun.

How hard would mother try
   To please her pretty lass?
Just as hard as the pattering showers
   Try to please the grass.

How fair does mother think
   The darling at her breast?
Just as fair as the glad white sea-bird
   Thinks the wave's white crest.

How long will mother's love
   For her treasure last?
Just as long as her heart keeps beating,
   Till her life be past.

How much will mother's love
   Change, as years are told?
Just as much as the mountain changes,
   Or the ocean old!

AT THE CLOSET-DOOR.

I 'M here at the closet-door, Lily:
  Mamma does n't know that I 'm here;
Your sobbing was truly so awful
  I thought I might comfort you, dear.

Now please don't imagine it 's merely
  To give you advice that I came;
Advice, when a body feels angry,
  Is like fuel added to flame.

And yet if you only will listen
  To three or four words, I am sure
The trial of asking for pardon
  Won't seem quite so hard to endure.

It is n't as if you were asking
  A stranger's forgiveness—ah, no!
Mamma would just die to defend you
  From harm, Lill; I 'm certain it 's so.

She suffers more deeply than you do—
  Believe it—in having you here.
There is n't a tear you are shedding
  That somehow don't cost *her* a tear.

And only because you are precious
  Your faults are things hateful to see ;
No buds will make beautiful roses
  Unless we give care to the tree.

Be good, and just ask mamma's pardon,
  Or else you 'll repent it, some day.
I 've been in dark closets myself, Lill ;
  Experience teaches, they say.

A SCHOOL-BOY OF THE PERIOD.

KING RICHARD THE THIRD? He ascended the
    throne
In the year—oh, pshaw, what a shame !
I knew it last night, sir ; 'pon honor I did—
  At any rate, Richard was lame.

It 's odd that I should not precisely recall
  The year he began, sir, to rule.
(Bill Jones, *can't* you tell me, or are you too mean?
  I 'll pay you for this after school).

He attained his position by what? Let me think.
  Oh ! murdering all of his kin.
His two little nephews were cruelly drowned
  In a hogshead of—was n't it gin ?

To whom was he married ? (Just whisper it, Bill,
    And I'll lend you my ball a whole day.)
To whom was he married, sir ? (Louder, Bill Jones,
    I can't hear a word that you say !)

How long did he reign ? Twenty years. (There's
    a guess !)
Who killed him—in what famous fight ?
Oh, yes, I remember ; the Black Prince, of course,
    At Hastings. (Bill, is n't that right ?)

Sufficient ? Detained after school, sir ! Well, well,
    The justice of that I *don't* see.
It 's enough to discourage (Stop giggling, Bill
    Jones !)
A hard-working student like me !

THE STAR'S STORY.

THERE dwelt a pure sweet star high up in heaven,
    That longed for something beautiful to love ;
And one fair night while gazing softly earthward,
    All from the blue tranquillities above,
She found a little gold-haired boy who slumbered,
    Gentle, and sinless as a new-born dove.

For many a night the star, with beamings tender,
  Shone through the quiet casement of the room
Where innocently slept her gold-haired darling,
  Compassed with utter silentness and gloom,
Until at last, yet watching him, she murmured :
  " He knows of my love, O weary doom !"

Then prayed the pure sweet star that God might
      change her
  To one of those glad fire-flies that flash bright
O'er meadowy lapses and low reedy marshlands,
  Through the long sombre watches of the night,
Dancing their dizzy dances, quaint and mirthful,
  Fandangoes and cachuchas of delight.

' For surely, then,' she thought, ' I shall be nearer
  Him whom my heart has learned to prize so well !'
And lo, the while she prayed her prayer, full fleetly
  Down through the gloaming's purple void she fell ;
Down to the meadow-lapses and green marshlands
  Where countlessly the sparkling fire-flies dwell.

Joyous it was to float on buoyant pinions
  Among those radiant multitudes, and seem
A new star in a new and nearer heaven,
  Her distant home viewed vaguely like a dream ;
Joyous it was, and yet not long she lingered,
  Idly among her brilliant peers to gleam,

'For I must gain,' she thought, 'my love's dim
    casement,
    Before the twilight darkens and he sleeps.'
Alas, poor fire-fly! journeying so hopeful,
    Her wings are tangled in the grassy deeps
That clothe a broad, still meadow, and she flutters
    Vainly to rescue what the strong grass keeps!

All night the cold dews chill her while she struggles,
    Bruising frail wings, frail body, and all night
Up from the gloomy sward come sudden flashes
    That pierce the solemn air with fitful light,
Till mournfully the flashes die forever,
    Just as the far dawn glimmers wild and white.

A GUARDIAN ANGEL.

You say that nobody has ever seen
A ghost, Mamma? I think that you are right.
People who die, as little Maudie died,
And dwell in Heaven and play on golden harps,
And float along with beautiful white wings,
Why should they ever ask to visit earth;
Even if God would let them? I believe
They do not come—except as Maudie comes,
Not seen, not heard, but somehow standing near

2

My bedside, on the nights of loneliest days,
When I have missed her, ah, *so* drearily !—
Remembering her glossy curls, her smile,
Her pretty ways, her cunning, gentle talk,
And how her warm, pink arms would clasp my neck
For good-night kisses.   Often I awake
And know, Mamma, that she is with me.   Morning
Has not yet broken, and the room is dark
And very still.   I listen for the sound
Of tiny feet upon the floor—the same
Whose steps made merry patterings long ago,
But stir not under those blue myrtles, now,
That tremble on her grave.   I listen,
But there is silence only.   Then I say
Softly, below my breath : " She is not here ;
She cannot come ; she is away with God."
And yet I listen, listen, till at last,
Longing to have her with me, in a voice
A little louder than before, I whisper :
" O Maudie, darling Maudie, are you there ?"
And then, it seems, a murmured answer comes,
Quite low and tremulous and musical,
As if an older, wiser Maudie spoke
Out from the shadows : " I am here ; I watch,
When you are sleeping, always by your bed.
I love you, I remember you ; I am
Your Maudie, just as in the other days."
O very sweet it is to hear those words,
And I am sure I do not fancy them,

Lying awake and shedding thankful tears,
And in the solemn darkness not afraid.

A LITTLE GIRL OF THE PERIOD.

THINK, Ada, how old we are growing!
    We 're both of us thirteen, my dear.
I 've almost decided not going
    To any more parties this year.

Now, love, I don't mean to turn preacher,
    And frown upon fashion ; but then
One feels like a very old creature
    With girls of eleven and ten.

I mean these young romps fresh and winning,
    With sleeve-loops and hair simply curled,
Their pleasure in life just beginning,
    Quite new to the ways of the world.

Ah, how they enjoy each flirtation,
    All flattery taking as truth !
Well, well ! they soon learn admiration
    Lasts only as long as their youth.

Of course we are foolish in sighing
    For joys that have vanished away.

One fact is beyond all denying—
Dear Ada, I 'm sadly *blasée*.

A LITTLE SAMARITAN.

WELL, Maudie, I trust that you 're better:
　I 've brought you some nice things from home;
Some jelly as clear as a crystal,
　Some pot-cheese as white as the foam.

And though your mamma has just told me
　You don't care to eat now you 're sick,
They 're still rather pleasant to look at,
　Like flowers that one must n't pick.

I hope you 'll be well for my party;
　Oh, Maudie, I should miss you so !
We 're going to have such lovely mottoes,
　And oceans of goodies, you know.

And then your new dress is quite ready;
　I shall not be jealous at all,
Though certain I am that you 'll prove, love,
　The recognized belle of the ball.

And now I 've some news for you, Maudie,
　It ought to delight you to hear.

Perhaps it will act—there 's no telling—
As sort of a remedy, dear.

I met Charley Williams last evening.
He bade me be sure to repeat
This kind little message he sent you :
I 'll whisper it—is n't that sweet?

Why, Maudie, you 're better already ;
That laugh had a clear healthy sound.
(There 's nothing like news from the friends they
love best
For bringing these sick people round).

ONE OF THESE DAYS.

ONE of these days, one of these days,
I shall wear a bonnet and a train, tra-la !
One of these days, one of these days,
I shall have a handsome watch and chain, tra-la !
Times will be nicer in many, many ways,
Easier, merrier, one of these days.

One of these days, one of these days,
I can go to bed when I 'm inclined, heigh-ho !
One of these days, one of these days,
I sha n't have my dresses hook behind, heigh-ho !

Times will be altered in many, many ways,
Doing as I wish to do, one of these days.

One of these days, one of these days,
Lessons will have ceased for good and all, tra-la!
One of these days, one of these days
I shall be the beauty of the ball, tra-la!
Times will have brightened in many, many ways,
Life will be jollier, one of these days.

One of these days, one of these days,
I shall be a lady like mamma, heigh-ho!
One of these days, one of these days,
I shall have a lover like papa, heigh-ho!
Times will be pleasant in many, many ways,
Living as I want to live, one of these days.

One of these days, one of these days,
Often do I dream of it in dreams, dear me!
One of these days, one of these days,
What a distant period it seems, dear me!
Time is very tardy in the working of his ways;
How I wish he'd hurry up "one of these days!"

IF.

IF I were a school-teacher, like Miss Snapp,
    And she were a scholar like me,
Oh, gracious! what lessons I 'd give her to learn,
    What sums in the Rule of Three!
And how, if she did n't forever behave
    In just the most saintly of ways,
Her ears should be slapped, and her buns locked up,
    And her recess ruined for days!

If I were as clever as Laura Sharp,
    And she were as stupid as I,
What thorough delight it would give me to act
    As monitor, meddler and spy!
And how I should tattle of all that she did,
    In Laura's contemptible style,
And smile, when she blundered at spelling or
        French,
    That horrid, unmerciful smile!

If I were a beauty like Rosa Bell,
    And she were a fright like myself,
What saucy remarks I should constantly make
    To vex her—the proud little elf!

What fun I should poke at her freckles, her nose,
   Her elbows, her knuckles, her hair,
And all with that delicate titter of hers,
   That stingingly lady-like air!

But then I am merely supposing, of course,
   Impossible things. Who can tell
What truly would happen if truly I were
   Miss Snapp, Laura Sharp, Rosa Bell?
Perhaps I should pity (revenge is so mean!)
   And help them and love them, all three,
And do unto others as I myself would
   That others should do unto me.

PARTING WORDS.

PLEASE, Mother dear, don't cry so; let me see
   On those pale lips, before the end, *one* smile.
Truly it would bring such great joy to me
   If I might have you glad a little while!

Only a little while before I go!
   Think, Mother, that it will not be for long;
Remember, too, I've seen God's lilies blow
   In dreams—in dreams have heard His angels' song.

Father is there and reaches loving hands !
I know it must seem lonelier when I leave,
But then there 's Katy still.   God understands
That which is best.   Be patient while you grieve.

Because you love me much I cannot doubt
It robs you of some pain to hear me say
My soul has not one fear to pass without
This little pallid fragment of frail clay.

And so take comfort.   Let these weak arms fold
The other glad, bright mother I once knew,
And think that when your time comes, Heaven
shall hold
Two more fond waiting hands to welcome you !

A LAMENTATION.

WHY is it I 'm always so busy
And never get anything done ?
I must have been born in a hurry,
I 'll die, it is certain, in one.

The girls that I know are not like me ;
There 's Alice and Jenny and Sue ;
They do all they ought, and have leisure
For quantities more than they do.
2*

And then they take matters so coolly,
  And live in so quiet a way;
But I 'm in perpetual fever
  And fluster the whole of the day.

And even at night very often
  I lie wide awake in my bed,
And thoughts of how much I 've neglected
  Are buzzing like bees in my head.

The lessons I 've studied to master
  And wretchedly failed in at school,
With many a dreary remembrance
  Of broken intention or rule.

Oh, dear, if I only knew some one
  Afflicted precisely like me,
Forever at work doing nothing—
  What excellent friends we should be !

A LITTLE MORALIST.

I 'M tired of fairy-books, Fanny,
  There is n't a word of them true ;
They 're simply not sensible reading
  For girls like myself and you.

Don't look so amazed; I mean it.
The fact of the matter is this:
We 've arrived at an age when common-sense
Is certainly not amiss.

For children like Will and Bessie
I suppose it is all very nice
To believe that a pumpkin was changed to a coach
And ponies were made out of mice;

Or that any one ever could manage,
Like Cinderella, to go
And dance at a ball in slippers of glass
That did n't get broken, you know.

Or that fairies have ever existed—
Live people with actual wings—
Who merely by waving their wands could perform
Such very remarkable things.

This is all nice enough for Bessie
And Will to believe in, I say;
But we, 't would be well to remember,
Are older and wiser than they.

And there seems to be so much, Fanny,
In this great, great world of ours,
Both real and beautiful besides,
Like sunsets and birds and flowers.

So much, mamma thinks, that was fashioned
  To charm and to teach us as well,
And stranger by far than the curious tales
  Those wonderful fairy-books tell ;—

So much we should value for being
  The blessings God renders his own,
That it 's better to love what is true, Fanny dear,
  And to leave what is false alone.

A "BOY" OF THE PERIOD.

I 'VE met the young creature you mean, Tom ;
  She 's truly quite pretty ; but then
We men of fifteen should look higher
  Than girls that have scarcely turned ten.

By Jove, it 's surprising how docile
  To female attractions you are ;
No, somehow life has n't yet made you
  Blasé—will you try a cigar ?

For my part, I seem to have grown, Tom,
  Quite callous to Cupid's worst stings ;
It may be my liver is ruined
  With parties and suppers and things.

Or yet it may be that I 'm reaching
    The sober, grave epoch in life
When, wearied with folly and pleasure,
    Men long for the joys of a wife.

And *apropos*, Tom ; that reminds me :—
    Kate Jones is a sweet little dear,
With charmingly kittenish manners
    And twenty-five thousand a year.

We 've danced lots of germans together
    And set people gossiping, too.
My chances look strong in that quarter ;
    I 'll make the attempt—would n't you ?

Yes, marriage is certainly better
    Than what is called bachelor-ease.
Is that brandy, Tom, on the table ?
    Just pour me a glass, if you please.

HARRY'S CURLS.

How glad, little Harry,
    Your hazel eyes glow,
As one after one, child,
    The sweet curls go !

You 're happy to part from
  This soft sunny hair
That made your wee shoulders
  So bonnily fair.

Perhaps papa 's right, dear ;
  You 're too old a boy
To wear these rich ringlets
  I wound with such joy.
So cut, cruel scissors,
  With sharp clicking sound,
As, ringlet by ringlet,
- They fall to the ground.

Ah, Harry, I envy
  Your light-hearted glee ;
It 's well to be merry—
  Mamma *cannot* be !
Each curl as it falls, dear,
  Is something that tells
Of drearier changes,
  More solemn farewells.

I see you so altered
  From what you are now,
With time 's many troubles
  To shadow your brow.
Believe it, my Harry,
  Whose laughter rings bold,

'T is not, after all, dear,
  Such fun to grow old!

I fancy the scissors
  That flash in my hand
Are working more mischief
  Than you understand.
Yes, love, with each ringlet
  So severed, I seem
To steal your life's sunshine
  In beam after beam!

THE WORST GIRL IN SCHOOL.

It's as easy for some kinds of people
  To always behave themselves well
As for churches to carry a steeple
  Or oysters to live in a shell;
But others are slower at seeing
  The virtue of method and rule;
I wish I could truly help being
  The worst girl in school.

Of course not a person believes me
  Whenever I say, in sad mood,
How greatly my wickedness grieves me
  And how I should like to be good.

But then my fibs are *so* disgusting ;
　　No wonder their treatment is cool :
It 's grown an old story, this trusting
　　The worst girl in school.

And yet I form each good intention
　　In excellent faith, do I not ?
But somehow I feel the prevention
　　Of something—it 's hard to tell what.
Perhaps of a wee impish fairy
　　That makes me her puppet and fool,
And laughs in her sleeve to see Mary
　　The worst girl in school.

It 's useless for teachers to drill me
　　With slaps and with lecturings now.
I cannot improve though they kill me ;
　　I honestly do not know how.
Miss Dragon's grim face seems all sinew,
　　Miss Gorgonclaw glares like a ghoul ;
But spite of hard looks I continue
　　The worst girl in school.

No doubt '*t would* be wiser than scold me
　　To kill such a living disgrace,
And set me where all could behold me,
　　Conspicuous in a glass case.
I might do some good as a warning
　　To other girls reckless of rule,

Seen ticketed thus every morning :—
" The Worst Girl in School."

THE ELVES.

When you hear, little folks, that the elves are no
    more,
Don t believe what the large people tell.
Less openly dwell they than ever before,
    But still among mortals they dwell.

And still, little folks, do they busy themselves
    In planning nice plans for you all,
And straight from their love, the benevolent elves,
    Does many a blessing befall.

Be sure they are watching you just as of old,
    When they watched the good children ; be sure
There is nothing so sweet for their eyes to behold
    As the faithful, the truthful, the pure.

And so, little folks, when you hear they are dead,
    Do n't believe what the large people say,
But try to deserve their sweet notice instead,
    And the elves will reward you, some day.

UNDER THE BED-CLOTHES.

I WOULD give so much now if I 'd only
　　Obliged dear mamma, and not read
That horrible ghost-story.　Gracious!
　　How strangely it runs in my head !

I 've crept deep down under the bed-clothes,
　　I 'm trying as hard as I can
To care not a bit for the darkness,
　　But just go to sleep like a man.

The story was nonsense, I 'm certain ;
　　Such things never happen, oh no ;
How queer that I should n't believe it,
　　And yet should be shivering so !

I 've counted a hundred and fifty,
　　But that does n't alter my fright.
I 'd rather have twenty good whippings
　　Than pass through another such night !

Of course I deserve to feel frightened :
　　Mamma was so careful to say :
" Remember, don't touch this book, Johnny,"
　　The morning she put it away.

And then like a bad, silly fellow,
  I read it all through on the sly—
Forgetting what God did to Adam
  When *he* disobeyed, by the bye.

THE ANGEL'S GIFT.

LAST night, while the world was sleeping,
  A beautiful angel came down,
Wearing a great gold cross on her breast,
  On her brows a lilied crown.

She passed full many a mansion
  Where slept the rich and the great,
Pausing at length by a cottage-door—
  A cottage of lowly state.

And there, in an humble chamber,
  She leaned o'er an humble bed,
Saying sweet words in a woman's ear,
  And these were the words she said :

" I have brought you a gift more costly
  Than jewels or gold could bring—
A gift you must keep, for Heaven's own sake,
  Beloved like a precious thing.

" For surely, if well you use it,
    This gift of mine shall become
A blessing whose worth no human lips
    Have power with words to sum."

Then the angel passed from the cottage,
    And starward his white wings spread,
While dawn, in the dim and distant east,
    Was staining the low skies red.

And ere that day's sun was risen
    The woman had seen with joy,
All sleepy and bonny and pink at her side,
    A wee little baby boy!

BROTHER WILLY.

WHITE little hands, where the white little roses
    Rest, looking not more white,
Lids that some strange long slumber closes
    Over the soft eyes' light;
Lips that seem done with smiles or sighing,
    Brow that the still hair screens,—
Do you all mean death?   But I stand here trying
    To puzzle out what death means.

Brother Willy is dead, they have told me—,
  Cannot laugh loud any more—
Cannot put forth pretty arms and fold me
  Close to his pinafore—
Cannot be mirthful and naughty and fearless—
' Cannot kiss great kisses, too.
Ah, brother Willy, such thoughts would be cheerless
  If I chose to think them of you !

Pshaw ! I won't think them. He 's not even sleeping ;
  He always was full of wild tricks.
Don't I remember the day he spent keeping
  Hidden among the hay-ricks ?
No, brother Willy, you cannot deceive me,
  Playing asleep as you are.
Open your eyes like a man ; and, believe me,
  You 'll just delight poor Mamma.

A GUILTY CONSCIENCE.

How mean of Mamma not to kiss me,
  Nor even to wish me good-night ;
Of course I was ugly this morning,
  And—all things considered—quite right.

Why could n't Mamma have allowed me
　　That candy I wanted for lunch?
There 's nothing so lovely in school-time
　　As cocoa-nut candy to munch.

But no; I could have bread-and-butter
　　And sponge-cake, and not a thing more,
And so I marched off in a tantrum;
　　I never was so mad before.

Mamma has been grim as a grave-yard
　　From that time to this.　And to-night
Just think of her not having kissed me!
　　She 's acting with horrible spite.

She 's looked very sad the whole evening;
　　Her eyes seemed so mournful and deep.
(There 's something all wrong with my pillow;
　　I somehow can *not* get to sleep!)

It 's horrid to be in the darkness
　　And think of how sad matters are;
Suppose I slip down to the parlor
　　And say a few words to Mamma.

Suppose I just tell her I 'm sorry;
　　I know she 'll forgive me, the dear!
Perhaps when I come back, my pillow
　　Won't feel half so hot and so queer.

CANDOR.

DID I know my French lesson at school to-day?
  I won't tell a story, Mamma:
I missed a whole verb from beginning to end—
  What horrid things those French verbs are!

Was I talkative? Why, to confess the truth,
  I did talk a very great deal.
It makes me feel sick to be silent, you know;
  My tongue's such a perfect mill-wheel.

Did I eat any lunch out of recess? you ask.
  Mamma, I'll speak truth and declare
That Emily Ludlow compelled me to take
  One half of a lovely ripe pear.

Was I tardy at school? Well, a little, Mamma,
  For what is the use to deceive?
The girls were through prayers when I got there,
        and, oh!
  'T was quite half-past nine, I believe.

Did I loiter at all in my journey to school?
  I see you're beginning to frown,
But the sum of the fact of the truth of it is:—
  I walked the whole way with Dick Brown.

A YOUNG POETESS.

I 'M going to try and write a little piece ;
　Of course I cannot write it very well.
I 'm going to say how fond I am of Spring,
　And tell whatever else I 've time to tell.

(Oh, gracious, I 'm afraid it won't be much,
　For poetry 's so dreadful hard to do !)
In Spring the bare, brown meadows all get green ;
　The skies (except on cloudy days) are blue.

The leaves begin to form upon the trees ;
　The buttercups and clovers blossom out.
The brooks are rather deep—and muddy, too,
　Which can't be very pleasant for the trout.

The orchards are all changed to snowy white,
　And many lovely birds are on the wing.
I think it might be stated that these birds
　Get married and have families in Spring.

For often you can find their little nests ;
　I found a wee one with four eggs in, once.
(Oh, dear, I can 't do poetry at all ;
　The only rhyme to finish with is—dunce).

FOR CHRISTMAS.

HEAP the logs and let the blaze
　　Crackle round their russet girth.
Fill to-day, of all your days,
　　With the merriest of mirth.
Life has cares enough, God knows,
　　Fate's demands are stern and drear ;
Yet for one day banish woes ;—
　　Christmas comes but once a year.

Draw the children round your knee,
　　Tell them, in the cosy room,
How Kris Kringle, quaint to see,
　　Issues from the chimney's gloom.
Share the happy games they play,
　　Give their little hearts glad cheer.
Love them with deep love to-day ;—
　　Christmas comes but once a year.

Men and women, girls and boys,
　　Make to-day a precious gem,
Bright, with golden household joys,
　　As the Star of Bethlehem !
Wear upon your brows love's sign,
　　As Christ wore it, pure and clear ;
Let your hidden goodness shine ;—
　　Christmas comes but once a year.

3

LOOKING SPRINGWARD.

Hot on the garden's mounded snow
  The sunbeams fall to-day,
And the icicle up at the roof is dripping
  Its diamond spear away.

The wind is damp and sharp, yet I feel
  In its touch no frosty sting—
The vaguest breath of a sweetness, rather,
  Like the promise of far-off Spring.

In a moment this delicate warmth may die,
  And cheerless gales be blown,
Trumpeting from the hills blue bastions
  That winter guards his own.

And the meadows by dusk may glisten chill,
  And the pane be pictured fair,
And to-night on its boughs a starlit cuirass
  The naked oak may wear.

But not with her happy dream, for this,
  Shall pleasured fancy part,
Believing the first glad thrill to have wakened
  Some violet's buried heart!

A COMFORT.

I SOMEHOW do not love the world as well,
    Now that dear Maudie is not here with me.
I think the same old sweetness does not dwell
    Anywhere just as it was wont to be.

Sometimes it seems as if the light winds said,
    When I take walks alone in field or lane :—
" Maudie 's asleep, with lilies round her head,
    Asleep, and will not ever awake again."

And sometimes, when a great gold bee flits by,
    Strange words seem spoken in his cheerful hum ·
" The lands are all so glossy-green—the sky
    So beautiful ; why does n't Maudie come ?"

And often, very often, I have dreams—
    Wide-awake dreams, by day—of how she sees
The flashes of the buttercups, the gleams
    Of swallows and the white-flowered elder-trees.

And that she walks, an angel, by my side,
    And loves me just as in those other hours
When she would call herself my little bride,
    And I would make her wreaths of elder-flowers.

This is my comfort.　For if she prefers
　To leave God's Heaven and join me here, sweet
　　　　pet,
Surely some day when I wear wings like hers,
　We shall be dearer friends than ever yet.

A PARTING.

WELL, Frankie, good-bye for the present;
　I hope you 've enjoyed yourself here.
You must make us another such visit,
　As long and as jolly, next year.

I 've heard that the city in summer
　Is always so horribly hot;
The change, I am sure, will be dreary,
　From country to town; will it not?

Are you truly quite sad about going?
　To judge from your looks, I should say
You would give a great deal to remain here
　For only a single short day.

But that is impossible, Frankie;
　Your trunk is all ready, you know,
And your mother has written, and—Goodness!
　I wish that you had n't to go!

I often shall think of you, Frankie,
  And miss you from morning till night.
Be careful to send me a letter
  As soon as you 've leisure to write.

A word or two more. You remember
  The day that we spent, you and I,
Alone in the woods with our luncheon,
  And something you said made me cry?

I thought what was asked very startling,
  And hurried away through the trees;
But now it 's all different, Frankie—
  I 'd *like* to be kissed, if you please.

"ALWAYS AS NOW."

I 'D have my darling
  Always as now;
Plump-cheeked and bright-eyed,
  Merry of brow.

I would not change him—
  No, no, not I;
Wishing my wee one
  Wee till I die.

Time that shall alter
    Cannot improve,
Cannot make fairer
    . This child of my love.

See the pink softness
    Of neck and arm ;
Change, touching either,
    Surely would harm.

Years, too, will darken
    His curls' warm gold.
Ah, that my darling
    Might not grow old !

Were he to-morrow
    In all mens' eyes
Lofty and honored,
    Famous and wise,

Rather than see him
    With crown on brow,
I 'd have my darling,
    Always as now.

THREE ROSES.

WHICH is the happiest rose to-day
  Of three that I know, I wonder?—
The rose at the window, the rose on the lawn,
  Or the rose in the meadow yonder?

Fair as a pearl is the face of one,
  While it dewily gleams and flutters
Close where its peaceful heart can hear
  What the peaceful household utters.

Velvet-petalled and crimson-hued,
  With mosses its stem enfolding,
One burns up from the flattered lawn,
  A marvel to all beholding!

And one on the barren meadow lives,
  Near a boulder huge and sullen;
A pale, wild thing, in a lonely world
  Of thistle and weed and mullein.

Happy those treasured garden-blooms,
  In their white and crimson graces,
But she of the meadow is happiest,
  Who looks but to God for praises!

EXCUSES.

I TRULY can't tell how it happened ;
  I meant to have studied them so ;
There wasn't a word in my lessons
  I hadn't intended to know.

As soon as school-hours were finished,
  Without the least bit of delay,
I hurried straight home, ('pon my honor !)
  Refusing to loiter or play.

I seated myself at the window,
  And took up my books like a man,
But over the way, on a sudden,
  The merriest organ began !

And such a ridiculous monkey
  Was making such glorious fun
That somehow I rushed for the sidewalk
  At far quicker speed than a run.

Perhaps you will scarcely believe it,
  (The fact was to me a great shock,)
But when I got back to my studies
  'T was dinner-time—just five o'clock !

I meant to work hard after dinner ;
  But what do you think happened then ?
Papa took us all to the circus ;
  We never got home till past ten.

Of course I slept quite late this morning ;
  And so you 'll excuse me, I trust ?
Kept in till I 've learned all my lessons !
  O goodness, how awful unjust !

A WISH.

How softly Spring enfolds it
  In films of tender grass ;
How lightly bend its violets
  When warm-breathed breezes pass ;
How clear its tiny headstone gleams,
  How clear and fair and still ;
How quiet is my darling's grave,
  Out on the quiet hill ;

I would that I might always keep
  This Spring-time round her tomb,
That grasses might not lengthen there,
  That roses might not bloom ;
3*

That splendid summer night not come,
  The flattered lands to fill,
Nor clovers gird my darling's grave,
  Out on the quiet hill.

But always I would have the skies
  Faint-blue, the sward faint-green,
And vistas of white-blossomed boughs
  Along the orchard seen ;
And pathos of the violets,
  And odors vaguely borne,
And Spring to mourn my darling,
  As only Spring can mourn !

AN ELYSIUM.

MAMMA, do you know what I really think
  The summit of all earthly bliss ?
No doubt you 'll be terribly shocked when you hear
  That simply and solely it 's this :

Nothing to do for a whole day long,
  No lessons, no errands at all ;
Grandma's big rocking-chair quite to myself ;
  And Puss on my lap in a ball.

Conveniently set on a table close by,
  Instead of my breakfast or lunch,
A plate of fresh toffy—the nice peanut sort—
  To munch, and to munch, and to munch!

And then to be reading a wonderful book
  As monstrous as Webster, (the bore!)
And crowded with fairy-tales, each that I read
  More sweet than the one read before.

Fine stories of dragons and wicked old queens
  And beautiful, ill-treated girls,
And splendid young princes with curls and blue
      eyes—
  Especially princes with curls.

And seated with Pussy in Grandma's big chair,
  Drawn up in a small cosy bunch,
'T would just be the summit of all earthly bliss
  To munch, and to read, and to munch!

A LITTLE RUNAWAY.

Where is our Freddy?—
  Mischievous Fred!
Nurse wants to find him;
  It's time for bed.

Cook, in the kitchen,
  Busy and hot,
Have you seen Freddy?
  " No I have not."

Jane, in the laundry,
  Washing away,
Have you seen Freddy?
  " No, not to-day."

John, in the garden,
  Weeding the flowers,
Have you seen Freddy?
  " No ; not for hours."

Gracious ! it 's bed-time.
  Where can he be?
Come, shaggy Carlo,
  Find him for me ! ·

Search through the barn-yard,
  Search here and there ;
Search well through the stable,
  Search everywhere.

Ah, search no longer ;
  Freddy is found—
In the gray pony's manger
  Slumbering sound !

A SCHOOL-GIRL OF THE PERIOD.

GEOGRAPHY? Yes, there's a lesson each day,
    But it's awfully hard to remember.
We've been in South Africa nearly a month;
    Perhaps we'll go north by November.

What history have we? It's quite a big book,
    Without any pictures—the bother!
To-day I was told I'd sustained a defeat
    In the Battle of—something or other.

Arithmetic? Oh, it's the bane of my life!
    No matter how hard I may study,
My knowledge of dividends, fractions and rules,
    Continues unchangeably muddy.

Proficient in spelling? I hope that I am,
    Though I shine less as writer than talker,
And don't mind confessing how often I use
    A pocket-edition of Walker.

I write compositions? Of course; once a week;
    We've *such* a dull subject to-morrow!
I manage to spin out a page and a half,
    Though lots of girls copy and borrow.

You ask me which lesson of all I prefer?
You'll think my reply most alarming.
In French we've a *gentleman* teacher, you know,
And somehow it's perfectly charming.

THE UNSOCIABLE COLT.

SHY little colt, here's a handful of clover;
Let us be friends, and begin from to-day.
Look, I am tall, and can reach the bars over;
Pretty brown frisker, don't gallop away.

I know if you'd wait but a minute to hear me
Without shooting off in such terrified style,
You would very soon make up your mind not to
fear me,
But listen until I had gossiped a while.

There's shaggy old Neptune—*he* thinks it no danger
To come when I call, but a matter of course.
Mamma says it's naughty to run from a stranger,
As I hope you'll agree, sir, before you're a horse.

Is that your mamma by the lily-pool yonder?
She is sleeker than you, and more gentle-eyed.
Is she scolding you now for bad conduct, I wonder,
In the whinny she gives as you bound to her side?

Well, Nep, let's be off in the woods for a ramble,
 And leave Master Colt to his own ugly mood.
I daresay he'll canter and frolic and gambol,
 Without the least sorrow for having been rude.

But one of these days, when his playtime is over,
 When he's broken to harness and whipt till he
  goes,
Perhaps he'll remember the handful of clover,
 And think what a blessing is kindness — who
  knows?

SCOLDING THE SEA.

OH, yes, you're very calm to-day,
 You broad, blue, brilliant sea—
Willing to let your breakers play
 Quite pleasantly with me.
And out where yonder pale gull dips,
 Where soft waves heave and swell,
Willing to bear the graceful ships
 As though you loved them well.

But I know who it was that made
 Such angry noise last night

Till, listening, I felt afraid,
  And shivered in my fright.
'T was you ; now don't deny it, pray,
  With that mild song you sing.
I don't believe a word you say,
  You great deceitful thing !

You may have done, for all I know,
  Some frightful mischief, too ;—
Have more dark secrets hid below
  That breast so bright and blue.
Perhaps poor sailors lost their lives
  To please your horrid spite ;—
Well, well ; you learned to widow wives,
  Old sea, before last night !

You 've lived so long, one might suppose
  You wise a little bit,
And able, when your temper rose,
  To keep a curb on it.
Does Father Neptune, standing by,
  Allow such capers ?   Ah,
Your ears would ache if you were I,
  And Neptune were Mamma !

I somehow can't but love you, though,
  Bad as your deeds may be,
For you 've such winning ways, you know,
  Beautiful, strong, strange sea !

Your mermaids must be happy girls,
  With not a thing to do
But float about in weeds and pearls
  And—Pshaw! you 've wet my shoe!

A DIALOGUE.

JOHNNY.

WHAT shall we do this fine morning?
  Shall we play hide-and-seek?
Shall we blow bubbles together?
Shall we go hunting for bird-nests?
  Lily, why don't you speak?

LILY.

Hide-and-seek, Johnny, is stupid;
  So, I think, bubbles are;
Then as for bird-nests, it 's wicked,
To touch them if even one finds them;—
  Besides, they are up so far.

JOHNNY.

Goodness! how lazy you 're getting.
  Laziness, Lill, is a sin.
Come, don't sit here in the orchard;
Let 's run a race to the mill-pond;
  I shall try hard not to win.

LILY.

Will you, indeed ?   How absurd, sir !
  Girls don't run races, you know ;
People will call me a hoyden ;
Not that I greatly should mind it,
  Only 't will grieve Mamma so !

JOHNNY.

Just as you please, miss.   However,
  What shall we do for our fun ?
Why are you smiling so queerly ?
Tell me now, Lill, what your thoughts are ;
  I 'll give a penny for one.

LILY.

Strangely enough, it has struck me
  That at some time in our life
Both you and I shall get married :
Let 's try the feeling beforehand ;
  Johnny, let 's play Man and Wife !

SUMMONED.

I HAD a vision last night, Mamma,
　When the room was vague and still,
And the low gold moon fell peacefully
　Behind the dead-black hill.
My eyes were open wide ;
　I am sure I did not sleep ;
And the night was solemn round my bed,
　And the silence very deep.

But suddenly it seemed, Mamma,
　That near the window, there,
The dark was blossoming flower-wise
　In bursts of sunny air.
And while I gazed and gazed,
　Clear amid girding gloom,
I saw, white-raimented and fair,—
　Can you not fancy whom ?

Yes, sister Isabel, Mamma—
　Lost, lovely Isabel !
And oh, the glory of her smile
　I have not words to tell !

She faded from my sight
    Before I dared to speak.
How much I would have given to leave
    One kiss upon her cheek !

Pray, do not turn your head, Mamma,
    But hold this pale, thin hand,
And promise to be brave when I
    Pass to the Heavenly land.
God sent our Isabel
    As messenger, last night.
Smiling, she spoke not, but I read
    Her quiet smile aright.

Only a little while, Mamma,
    And we shall meet once more,
To clasp white hands of welcoming
    Upon the peaceful shore.
Weep but a few sad tears
    Over my short farewell ;
Remember that the amaranth blooms
    After the asphodel !

BLIGHTED FLOWERS.

THIS morning when I came among the flowers,
 The flowers that to tend were my delight,
A chilling change had touched them through the
  watches,
 The watches of the frosty Autumn night;
And mournfully I looked upon their faces,
 Their faces dim and piteous with blight.

" Oh, surely," to my heart in grief I whispered,
 I whispered so my heart alone could hear,
" The sorrowful Death-Angel, while we slumbered,
 We slumbered, heart of mine, and had no fear,
About our precious flower-land has wandered,
 Has wandered and has left its beauties drear."

And then it seemed as if my heart made answer,
 Made answer sweetly, softly : " Months ago
Along these very paths we came, one morning,
 One morning when you bade me thrill to know
That bounteously your crocuses had blossomed,
 Had blossomed in a golden overflow.

"And 'surely,' I remember that you whispered,
   You whispered by the glowing garden-plot,
'The radiant Life-Angel, as we slumbered,
   We slumbered, heart of mine, and knew it not,
About my precious flower-land has wandered,
   Has wandered and has glorified the spot.'"

"Dear heart," I said, "consoling hope thou lendest,
   Thou lendest faith, while dismal winter lowers,
And biddest me devoutly to be mindful,
   Be mindful that among these ruined bowers
The radiant Life-Angel yet shall wander,
   Shall wander, re-illumining my flowers!"

ASPIRATIONS.

Look at the moon, like a great red plum,
   Just where the sky commences.
Goodness, how jolly to jump on her top
   And sail over houses and fences!
Higher and higher and higher to sail,
   Danger delightfully scorning,
Sure she would bring me at last, good moon,
   Safe back to earth in the morning.

Fancy how nice to be near some star,
  And find out what it was made of!
Except for the danger of falling off,
  How little to feel afraid of!
Higher and higher float on, red moon,
  Up in the dim sky far go ;
Yours were a merrier trip, to-night,
  With merry me for a cargo!

THE LITTLE CRIPPLE.

Yes, Katy, I felt bitter when first came
  The knowledge of how all was different
From those bright times before God made me lame ;
  But now (believe it, Katy,) I 'm content.

I don't mean, dear, that if I rose and found,
  Some morning, I could walk without distress,
Needing no crutch, and was quite strong and sound,
  I should n't cry aloud for thankfulness.

Ah, no—not that! But, Katy, I just mean
  That somehow it has pleased God, good and wise,
To make the earth I live in grand and green,
  To bend above it beautiful blue skies ;

To have glad-colored flowers in many a place,
  And shining rivers and blithe singing brooks,
To fill His lovely world with light and grace
  And bird-songs, through its countless happy
  'nooks

And He has done this much that I may be
  Sure of His love. And, Katy, I am sure.
All that He asks for in return from me
  Is only with firm courage to endure.

Suppose some friend should give you gifts most
    fair,
  Withholding for himself some gift apart.
Because he had withheld that, would you care
  To call him pitiless and hard of heart?

Of course you would n't, Katy. So with me.
  I have the grass and flowers and skies and birds.
God has been very kind, and therefore He
  Deserves my gratitude in deeds and words.

And though I felt so bitter when first came
  The knowledge of how all was different
From those bright times before God made me lame,
  Now, Katy, I 've grown cheerful and content.

IN SICKNESS.

'T IS sweet to know of clear, soft Spring's returning,
Though I must lie so still and play no more,—
Not mark the bounteous crocus-bushes burning,
Not mark the merry swallows flash and soar.

'T is sweet to think, although my room be darkened,
That heaven outside is rich with wooing sun,
And that the pure, shy blooms of May have heark-
ened
Heaven's beautiful persuasions, one by one.

While often gleam the faces loved right dearly,
From shadow, and while gleam caressing hands,
This single joy is evident most clearly,
That Spring re-welcomes the delighted lands.

Yet they who will not let the perfumes find me,
Nor any glimmer of the altered air,
Remember too much glory would but blind me,
Are heedful what my poor weak frame can bear.

Still, I take comfort. There are flowers blowing,
And there are flowers that will blow ere long.
Shall I not trust these latter wait my knowing,
And hide their loveliness till I am strong?

4

Or shall I only deem myself some flower
 That cannot bloom, while its fond sisters call,
A little fearful, in this golden hour,
 Lest it shall gain no grace to bloom at all?

APPLE-GATHERERS.

Down many an orchard-row
 The luscious apples glow,
This merry Autumn morning, fresh and bright.
 And on the frosted grass,
 Gold and scarlet as we pass,
Lie the beautiful rich wind-falls of last night.

Let us fill the baskets well,
 Harry, Frank and Isabel,
With greening, russet, pippin and the rest.
 We're not very strong, it's true,
 But can help by what we do,
Provided we resolve to do our best.

And suppose we promise, all,
 That no apple, large or small,
Shall tempt us into eating it until
 Our work is wholly done,
 And we've leisure for the fun
Of walking round and eating to our fill.

Don't you think that right and fair?
Goodness gracious! I declare
Here's a tempter rosy-cheeked enough to kiss!
After all, the better plan
Is to gather what we can,
And commence to eat immediately—like this.

CLEOPATRA.

WE'VE called our young puss Cleopatra;
  'T was Grandpa who named her like that.
He says it means lazy and idle—
  A queer enough name for a cat!

But then she is certainly idle,
  And lazy besides, beyond cure;
And if this is the word's definition,
  It's better than Tabby, I'm sure.

She leads the most lovely existence,
  And one which appears to enchant,
Asleep in the sun like a snow-flake
  That tries to get melted and can't;

Or now and then languidly strolling
  Through plots of the garden to steal

On innocent grasshoppers, crunching
  Her cruel and murderous meal ;

Or lapping from out of her saucer—
  The dainty and delicate elf !—
With appetite spoiled in the garden,
  New milk that 's as white as herself.

Dear, dear ! Could we only change places,
  That do-nothing pussy and I,
You 'd find it hard work, Cleopatra,
  To live, as the moments went by.

Ah, how would you relish, I wonder,
  To sit in a school-room for hours ?
You 'd find it less pleasant, I fancy,
  Than murdering bugs in the flowers.

JEALOUS OF BABY.

IT 's not very difficult, Bessy,
  To tell what you 're grieving about.
Those frowns are quite easy to fathom,
  And so is that terrible pout.

You 're jealous of Baby; I know it.
  Why, Bess, you 've been looking forlorn,
And serious as a sexton,
  Since dear little Baby was born.

Just stand with me now by her cradle,
  Where, sleeping so softly, she lies,
Her pretty pink mouth like a rose-bud,
  The satin lids veiling her eyes.

Pray, answer me—is n't she charming?
  And gentle? and pure as a dove?
Ah, Bess, can you blame us for loving
  What God surely meant us to love?

And why should you think yourself slighted,
  Not tenderly prized any more?
Believe it, you 're still just as precious
  To all of our lives as before.

Come, kiss and make friends with the Baby;
  You 'll find her so pleasant to kiss.
I know you have love enough hid in your heart
  To spare a wee darling like this!

OUR BENNY.

A SONG for our Benny, our fine five-year-older,
  Our imp of all mischief and fun,
With plump little arm and with pink little shoulder
  And ringlets that rival the sun.

A song for our Benny who never is quiet,
  Our wild, unrestrainable lad,
The spirit of clamor and frolic and riot,
  The vixen of all that is bad.

A song for our Benny, and grave be the verses
  Wherein his dark deeds we enroll;
How right from his heart he abominates nurses
  And grandly disdains their control.

A song for our Benny, tormentor of Baby,
  A true household terror, I vow;
So bad that one shudders to think what he may be,
  A Nero in petticoats now.

A song for our Benny, whose bad acts are thirty
  To one that is good, all declare;
With face and with hands irreclaimably dirty,
  And tangled, uncombable hair.

A song for our Benny; 't is certain we owe him
  A whipping—that matter 's quite clear ;
And yet . . . I defy any mortal to know him
  And not fall in love with the dear !

REMEMBERING.

IT seems very strange and lonely, Mamma,
  Not to have Nellie here
In these happy mornings of May-time,
  The brightest and best of the year !

She so loved the white of the orchards, Mamma,
  The gold of the crocuses, too,
And the blue of the violets, colored
  To match her own eyes' gentle blue.

And don't you remember last May-time, Mamma,
  Her roguish, rare, merry delight
To find a bird's-nest in the lilacs,
  With four cunning eggs, brown and white ?

And then how the butterflies pleased her, Mamma !
  She never would chase them, would Nell.
The largest and least of God's creatures
  Our darling loved equally well !

What melodies breathed in her laughter, Mamma,
    What innocence dwelt on her face!
And though her form's grace was quite perfect,
    Her soul had a lovelier grace!

I know she is happy in God's other world,
    But ah, if he spared her in this
For just a sweet moment each morning—
    The time that it takes for one kiss!

IN AUTUMN WEATHER.

ALTHOUGH these cool winds have a lonely sigh,
    Sad, when I listen, as a tolling bell,
I think the summer must be glad to die
    And bid her flowers and foliage farewell.

For are not all the meadows bright indeed
    With stalks on stalks of gaudy golden-rod?
Does not the elder wear its purple bead
    And many a beautiful dark aster nod?

Yes, summer surely is right glad to go.
    Among the maple's crimson-mottled leaves
And in the lofty chestnut's brilliant glow
    There is no sign of anything that grieves.

Ah, well, perhaps she is so glad because
   God has made some sweet promise to her here,
And she delights that its fulfilment draws
   With every moment nearer and more near.

Some promise about seeing, when she dies,
   All her lost children of those earlier hours ;
The spirits of her vanished butterflies
   And sweet wee angels made from her dead
      flowers !

BRAVE RESOLVES.

WELL, Katy, so you 've come to spend the day, dear?
   Let me put your cloak and bonnet on the bed.
A very pretty bonnet, by the way, dear ;
   I think that your complexion favors red.

And, Katy, now for twelve delightful kisses,
   The heartiest and warmest you can show :
No need, of course, to mention, love, that this is
   My birthday, since you knew it long ago.

How time is slipping, Katy ! Have you ever
   Really thought what grown-up girls we are, we
      two ?
I wonder if we ought appear more clever,
   And act a little less as children do.
     4*

I 've somehow been reflecting on it, lately.
  Suppose we make a promise, you and I,
Hereafter, dear, to care not quite so greatly
  For games and toys and candy.   Shall we try?

I see you 've brought your doll with you. How
         pleasant,
  If only there was mine to play with, too !
I 've asked Mamma to keep it—for the present.
  Perhaps you don't believe me, but it 's true.

Yes, dolls, you know are certainly not suited
  To girls that in a year will be thirteen.
O *what* a cunning cap, all trimmed and fluted !
  Why, Katy, she 's a perfect little queen !

I fear it 's rather stupid work, this trying
  To seem so very dignified and cold.
It almost makes a body feel like crying
  And wishing she were young instead of old.

My birthday might have been so nice and jolly
  And now there 's hardly anything to do.
I 've half a mind to ask Mamma for Dolly
  Just this one single morning.   Would n't you ?

TIRED OUT.

Quite wearied with your toys and sports,
  While evening shades grow deeper,
You nestle in the arm-chair's lap,
  A bonny little sleeper.
Across your tangled golden curls
  The mellow light is falling;—
O sleep and rest while glooms the west
  And katydids are calling.

About the house the whole day long
  Your happy voice has sounded;
Here on the rocking-horse you leapt,
  Here up the stair-case bounded.
Now teasing Baby into shrieks,
  Now grand with pipe and bubble,
But somehow yet the household pet,
  In spite of all your trouble.

O merry-maker blithe and bold,
  With pranks we could not number,
At last your fun has found an end
  In harmlessness of slumber!
Kind nurse will shortly steal to bear
  The truant rogue she misses,
Where dawn shall shed upon his bed
  The brightness of her kisses.

With mirth and mischief once again
  Our boy shall greet us, after
The rose has freshened on his face,
  The music in his laughter.
So sleep and rest, our loveliest,
  Till matin lights be slanting ;
O sleep and rest, while glooms the west
  And katydids are chanting.

THE CHRISTMAS-TREE.

CROWD in, merry little ones ; gleaming with tapers
  The Christmas-Tree greets you at last.
Behave yourself, Bessy ; and Harry, no capers ;
  And Willy, don't hurry so fast.

Believe me, there 's plenty of time to take matters
  Quite coolly and calmly, my dears ;
Remember that clothes can be torn into tatters
  And screams are not good for old ears.

Well, is n't it beautiful ?   Gracious, how pleasant
  Your marvelling glances to view !
Yes, somewhere among those bright boughs there's
      a present
  For you, and for you, and for you !

And so Bessy thinks it a wonderful cedar;
  She 'd just like to climb it, the elf!
And wee Kitty questions, with no one to heed her—
  " Did Santa Claus light it himself?"

And Harry discovers the top he 's been yearning
  To buy for a fortnight and more ;
And sharp-eyed young Willy already is burning
  To flourish his new battledore.

Now, children, quite quietly, just as you 're bidden,
  Come stand beside Grandma and me,
While Father shall show you what treasures lie
      hidden
  For all in the gay Christmas-Tree.

LITTLE ISABEL.

A BLUE midsummer twilight. Day had set,
  And soft winds made the garden leafage stir,
Sending sweet wafts of rose and mignonette
  In through the still room where we watched by
      her.

A single great gold star was hanging clear
  Over the damask sunset. We knew well
That sure as even this star must disappear,
  So death must soon find little Isabel.

And now the west grew paler and the star
  Sank lower, lower, and the night was come.
Through the wide-open window, seen afar,
  We watched those glooming heavens, white-faced
    and dumb.

Presently little Isabel's weak hand
  Moved gently, and she named a name. At this—
A summons more than any king's command—
  Two lips met hers in a strong eager kiss.

Just then behind some dead-black distant trees
  The star dropt, hidden wholly.   While it fell
There came a long wild murmur of the breeze,
  And peace was with our little Isabel.

OUR QUEEN.

PERHAPS there are many as lovely as she ;
  I doubt it, you 'll pardon my stating.
This babe is the princess of babes unto me,
Her rattle for sceptre, for throne my knee,
  And Nurse for the Lady in Waiting.

To us, who obey them with untiring zeal,
 Her mandates are issued serenely.
Gug-gug is a *fiat* that knows not repeal,
Coo-coo is a praise of her courtiers leal,
 In tones condescendingly queenly.

Her bath is a question of state. 'T is a sort
 Of treason to break her siesta.
Papa, at his sovereign's tyrannical court,
Assumes, by the right of a genius for sport,
 The *rôle* of Her Majesty's Jester.

Receptions of Grandma, when visiting town,
 Are held amid pomp rarely splendid.
In radiant ribbons and costliest gown,
(God gave her those tiny bright curls for a crown,)
 The greeting is grandly extended.

Her personal income of corals and caps
 Quite equals her royal position.
The rule of her nursery suffers no lapse ;
An absolute monarchy, tempered with naps,
 It meets an unvaried submission.

Like that of all despots, her reign is not free
 From faults, I am candid in stating ;   [be ?—
Yet who such a despot's proud slave would not
Her rattle for sceptre, for throne my knee,
 And Nurse for the Lady in Waiting.

A CRADLE SONG.

O SLUMBER, my darling; the white star is beaming
   From pale yellow dusk in the west.
O slumber, my darling; with beautiful dreaming
   Its gleaming shall dower thy rest.

O slumber, my darling; the white star is glowing
   Leagues out on the shadowy sea,
And if the wild winds there be drearily blowing
   The knowing is not unto me.

O slumber, my darling; the white star in pillows
   Of purple-hued cloud sinks to sleep!
This gale that is tossing the poor faded willows,
   Wakes billows afar on the deep!

O slumber, my darling; the white star is dying,
   The gold Autumn gloaming is dim;
My thoughts to thy mariner-father are flying,
   And, sighing, I fear me for him.

O slumber, my darling; the white star is beaming
   No longer, and vague is the light.
Perhaps where the grave of thy father is gleaming,
   Are screaming the sea-gulls to-night.

SANTA CLAUS.

HE journeys a guest
To our gladdened west,
In the gay memorial season,
At the merry time of chime and rhyme,
When pleasure romps with reason.

Strange tales we know
Of his beard of snow
And the reindeer-steeds that draw him,
But never a man there lives who can
Affirm that he ever saw him.

Always he pays,
In secret ways,
Those visits that delight us,
And drops by stealth his Christmas-wealth,
Too cautious to affright us.

And though unseen,
Where his hands have been
Rare gladness follows after,
While his praises float from many a throat
In ripples of mellow laughter.

To us his name
Means more than fame,
With fairest memories round it ;
He loveth well the Christmas-bell,—
O bid our steeples sound it !

And warm and free
Let the greeting be
As the flames of our brightest ingle ;
For he comes a guest whither every breast
Pays homage to Kris Kringle !

AT THE WINDOW.

How nice it is to watch beside the window
    The pleasant sights that one may often see !
I mean a body who has lots of leisure,
    And is n't always hard at work like me.
(Seven and five are twelve, and eight are twenty ;
    Add three more, carry two and set down three.)

O what a cunning treasure of a baby !
    It looks like that new crying-doll of mine.
And how its pretty French nurse seems to love it !
    It must be very rich to dress so fine.
(Two and nine are eleven, and eight added [nine.)
    Make nineteen ; two more fives make twenty-

Mamma is going out with sister Rachel.
  O dear! if I could only go ; but then
I merely am a wretched little school-girl,
  And Rachel's big, and flirts with gentlemen.
(Add two to six, and that is eight ; and two more
  Make ten ; and add a pair of nines to ten.)

Before I get to be a grown young lady
  There are so many stupid years to meet!
O there's an organ-grinder and a monkey ;
  Isn't the monkey's jacket just *too* sweet?
(Add up the sum's last column quite correctly,
  And when it's finished—run across the street.)

A PRAYER TO SUMMER.

BEAUTIFUL SUMMER, stay with us always ;
Never fly back among distant lands.
Look : to the clear-blue heavens above me
I, little Betty, lift pleading hands!

Stay with us, Summer, and keep sweet roses
Year after year still glowing bright!
Pink ones, pale ones and velvety crimsons,
Where the bee booms in delight!

Don't let the harsh loud winds, dear Summer,
Ruin your hollyhocks' fair proud heads.
Don't let the desolate rain fall bleakly
On the poor pansy-beds!

Have n't you any deep love for your children,
Gay flowers, bonny birds, twinkling leaves?
Shall you not grieve when you wish them farewell,
Just as a mother grieves?

How much pleasanter not to have snow-flakes
Cover the world from east to west,
Making it sombre and dreary—filling
The black-bird's empty nest!

Beautiful Summer, stay with us always!
Never fly back among distant lands!
Look: to the warm blue heavens above me,
I, little Betty, lift pleading hands!

AUTUMN.

WHEN dawn breaks chill the birds are still—
   Not a wee numb throat that twitters—
And meshed in the grasses, pearl on pearl,
   The marvellous hoar-frost glitters.

The sun rides up and the hollyhock's cup
    Has lost its crimson wassail,
And the poppy stirs a ruined crest
    And the corn a blighted tassel.

A sharp wind tears the pippins and pears
    Off branches, onward sweeping ;
The plump peach drops, the ivory gourds
    Through wilted leaves are peeping.

O'er meadowy ways there floating strays
    A silken fleece of thistles,
And the swarthy chestnut's emerald husk
    In lane and pasture bristles. ·

To a sound of sighs the fair year dies
    And the brief day waxes older,
And every gust that strips the pomp
    From the gaudy wood, is colder.

Now twilight falls, and the chamber walls
    Grow dim and the white stars glisten,
And out in her gloom the katydid calls,
    For lonely hearts to listen.

AN AWAKENING.

HERE, Susie, take my paper-dolls,
   My Rollo books, my games;
I 'm getting old enough to make
   An end of trivial aims.
For very naturally now
   My inclination leans
Toward the sensible pursuits
   Of people in their 'teens.

Henceforward I shall play a part
   More fitting to my years;
One cannot always be a child
   Like you, love, it appears.
This life of ours, perhaps you 've thought,
   Has many changing scenes,
And children are *so* different
   From people in their 'teens!

My dresses must be longer, now,
   Than I am used to wear;
Mamma of course will furnish me
   A net for this wild hair;
And as for high-necked pinafores
   And sleeve-loops, reds or greens,
They 've much too juvenile an air
   For people in their 'teens.

And, Susie, I shall cease to buy
  Molasses-drops ; they soil
One's fingers, and one's appetite
  Unquestionably spoil.
Those two stiff Tompkins girls next door,
  As proud as little queens,
Will soon discover I have grown
  Like people in their 'teens!

And lastly, I have half a mind,
  If ever Charley Brown
Should join me in the street again,
  Rather to smile than frown.
His company, you know, I don't
  Dislike, by any means,
And bashfulness does *not* become
  Young ladies in their 'teens.

FINIS.